Contents

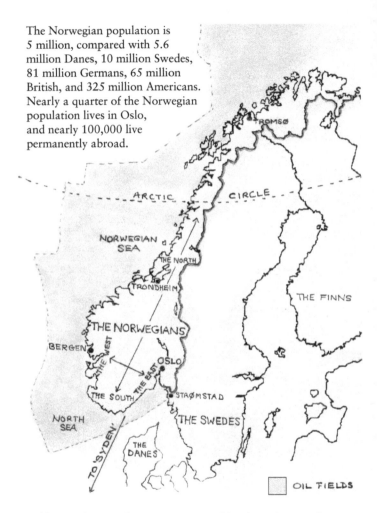

The Norwegian population is 5 million, compared with 5.6 million Danes, 10 million Swedes, 81 million Germans, 65 million British, and 325 million Americans. Nearly a quarter of the Norwegian population lives in Oslo, and nearly 100,000 live permanently abroad.

TROMSØ

ARCTIC CIRCLE

NORWEGIAN SEA

THE NORTH

TRONDHEIM

THE FINNS

THE NORWEGIANS

BERGEN

THE WEST

OSLO

THE SOUTH THE EAST

STRØMSTAD

NORTH SEA

THE SWEDES

TO SYDEN

THE DANES

OIL FIELDS

Norway is a very long country, stretching from the top of Europe to the Arctic Circle. If you stuck a (very large) pin in Norway's southern-most point and spun the country round, it would reach all the way to Italy.

Xenophobe's®
guide to the
NORWEGIANS

Dan Elloway

Xenophobe's Guides

Published by Xenophobe's® Guides.
Web site: www.xenophobes.com
E-mail: info@xenophobes.com

Printed 2018

Editor – Catriona Tulloch Scott
Series Editor – Anne Tauté
Cover designer – Vicki Towers
Map – Jim Wire
Printer – CPI Antony Rowe, Wiltshire

Cover: The image of a beautiful *bunad*
is reproduced by kind permission of
Norske Bunader Oslo AS / norskebunader.no.
The smiling troll with the Norwegian flag
is ©Sergii Mostovyi and the mittens are
Norwegian Selbu mittens.

ePub ISBN: 9781908120694
Mobi ISBN: 9781908120700
Print ISBN: 9781906042431

Nationalism & Identity

Norwegians define themselves in simple terms: they are not Swedish. This simple definition comes from centuries of being dominated both politically and culturally by the Swedes, and millions of foreigners believing Norway to be the capital of Sweden (it's not, just in case you are unsure).

> **66 Norwegians define themselves in simple terms: they are not Swedish. 99**

To show the world that they are Norwegian and definitely not Swedish, every Norwegian, at any moment in time, will be wearing an item of clothing with a Norwegian flag on it.

How Norwegians see themselves

Once a Norwegian has established that he or she is not Swedish, their identity follows strict geographical rules. To the world, they are Europeans. To the Europeans, they are Scandinavians. To the Scandinavians, they are Norwegians. To other Norwegians, they are from the East or West coast. To anyone from the (East or West) coast, they are from a tiny island somewhere off that coast.

This island will usually have its own dialect, spoken by only the few thousand native islanders, its own football team and often its own single-person police force. Most Norwegians are very proud of their own little island, but they will still move away as soon as they are old enough.

There is a distinct split between the East and West coasts in Norway, emphasised by the very different dialects and by the distance between the two. It's a nine-hour drive from Oslo in the East to the city of Bergen in the West. Taking in two mountain passes, the journey can last considerably longer when snow closes the road to anything but 'column driving', when cars have to wait at the foot of the mountain for a snow plough and then follow the plough across the mountain in a long column.

> **❝ People on the West coast claim that the city of Bergen is their capital – as opposed to the official capital of Oslo, in the East. ❞**

People on the West coast claim that the city of Bergen is their capital – as opposed to the official capital of Oslo, in the East. There are even two 'national' newspapers, one published in Bergen and the other in Oslo. Both newspapers report national and international news, but largely ignore any events happening on the other side of the country.

People from the West think of Easterners as soft, self-obsessed and urban (which has negative connotations in nature-loving Norway), while people from the East refer to Westerners as insanely chatty, boastful and provincial. However, when he looks North, it

2

does not matter if a Norwegian is from the East or West. Because, when he looks North, he is definitely from the South.

Northern Norway, which stretches up into the Arctic Circle, is a region in itself. People from the North are hardy, silent folk who spend half the year hunting, skiing and fishing in complete darkness. They think all Southerners, whether from the East or West coast, are soft suburban types. Southerners, for their part, are convinced all Northerners have been driven slightly crazy by the midnight sun.

> **It does not matter if a Norwegian is from the East or West. Because, when he looks North, he is definitely from the South.**

The North includes around 70,000 Sami, the original indigenous people of Scandinavia. The Sami population stretches across the Arctic Circle, taking in Norway, Sweden, Finland and Russia. In the 1980s the Norwegian government passed laws that protected the Sami culture, language and way of life. Most Norwegians feel the Sami are essentially a separate nation living, for the most part, on Norwegian soil. The Sami tend to feel the same way.

When pushed, a Norwegian will describe himself as shy, hard-working and nature-loving. This is accurate, to an extent. A Norwegian is extremely shy, until he gets two drinks inside him, at which point he will talk to anyone he meets. He works extremely hard until the clock hits 4 pm, at which point he will switch off his computer and go home. And all Norwegians love nature, especially when trying to despatch it with a hunting rifle.

17 May, National Day

The Norwegians are proud of their land, with its stunning fjords and endless forests. They are proud of their government, national skiing team and education system. They are even proud of their high tax rate. They are, in short, proud to be Norwegian. But they do not like to shout about it, even though they sometimes can't help themselves. The shouting happens most obviously on 17 May, Norwegian National Day.

On 17 May 1814 the founding fathers of modern Norway, the *Eidsvollsmenn* (literally, the Men of Eidsvoll) signed Norway's constitution at the manor house in Eidsvoll. The constitution was considered to be one of the most democratically liberal in the world. However, at the time Norway was under Danish rule and the constitution was seen as a declaration of independence. From that day onwards, Norwegians have gathered on 17 May to express their nationalism, even though Norway was later ceded to Sweden and only gained independence in 1905.

66 The Norwegians are proud to be Norwegian. But they do not like to shout about it, even though they sometimes can't help themselves. 99

17 May is the most important day in the Norwegian calendar. It's a day of children's parades, flag waving, eating and drinking. For a few hours, once a year, the entire country is draped in the Norwegian colours of red, blue and white. In small villages, along fjords and mountain valleys, children march waving flags and people greet each other by saying 'Gratulerer med dagen' (Congratulations for the day). In Oslo, the parade winds past the palace and the Royal Family stands for hours waving to the passing crowds. These celebrations even take place outside Norway. As long as there are more than two Norwegians, they will have a parade.

> 66 For a few hours, once a year, the entire country is draped in the Norwegian colours of red, blue and white. 99

17 May is seriously hard work for parents. The day starts at 8 am with (simulated) canon fire to wake up any parents who have slept through the alarm. By this time most parents have already raised the national flag on the flagpole in the garden and decorated the balcony and porch with mini paper flags. They then dress the family in their Sunday best – either a *bunad*, the traditional, intricately-embroidered, national costume, or a suit with a ribbon in the colours of the national flag pinned to the lapel – and drive to a friend's house for breakfast. As soon as breakfast is finished, it's back in the car to deliver the children to

school, and then a quick jog to 'book' a decent spot along the parade route. They then stand for three or four hours waving flags as every school class and brass band in the district passes by playing music and carrying banners, before they can finally relax with a *pølse* (sausage) and *softis* (soft ice-cream).

Despite the outward show of nationalism, 17 May is not a celebration of national power. There are no military displays or parades of tanks and troops, and there are no speeches celebrating victories over oppressors. 17 May is a celebration of unity, a show of pride in a nation where everyone works towards the same goals. It's about a country of loners coming together to celebrate what they can achieve when they work together as a community – and Norwegians are as proud of 17 May as they are of their nation.

> **❝ Although they will never say it, all Norwegians feel slight pity for anyone from another country. ❞**

How Norwegians see others

Although they will never say it, all Norwegians feel slight pity for anyone from another country. The Norwegians believe all other countries are less beautiful and more heavily populated than their own, which means people living in these countries are not able to be alone in nature very often. For any Norwegian, this is a very sad state of affairs.

To a Norwegian, a lack of spacious countryside equals urbanity – and Norwegians are suspicious of urban culture, especially foreign urban culture. It is, they think, a den of sinful behaviour where people sit around in cafés drinking coffee and achieving nothing, and, for Norwegians, achieving nothing is the biggest sin of all.

> **A lack of spacious countryside equals urbanity – and Norwegians are suspicious of urban culture.**

This misconception is reinforced by the fact that Norwegians holiday every summer in resorts packed to the brim with other Norwegians. These holidays are usually in *Syden* ('the South') which is the all-encompassing term for southern Europe that makes no attempt to distinguish between the different countries, cultures or languages. In fact, the only thing important about *Syden* is that it is South of Norway, and hot.

How Norwegians think others see them

Norwegians believe that no-one outside Scandinavia knows the difference between any of the Scandinavian countries. (They are usually right in this belief.) They are also convinced that every foreigner thinks that Norway is the capital of Sweden. (They are often right in this belief, too.)

Outwardly, the Norwegians do not seem to mind

7

that the rest of the world thinks their country is a city in Sweden. 'It's a small country,' they say to each other, 'why should anyone know who we are?' But inwardly, Norwegians find this situation quite annoying. 'We may be a small country,' they think to themselves, 'but we are at least as important as Sweden.'

If someone does know the difference between Norway and Sweden, a Norwegian will immediately assume the worst. 'Please, no Viking and troll jokes,' he will say, before proceeding to list as many jokes about Vikings and trolls as he can, simply happy that a foreigner does not think he is Swedish.

Character

To understand the Norwegian character, you first have to understand the geography. Norway is not just a big country with a small population. It's a big country with a small population that is exceptionally inconvenient to travel around. Because of the fjords and mountain ranges, most roads, except a few highways in and out of the big cities, are single lane. Even the trains often run on just one track and have to stop in passing places to allow trains travelling in the other direction to get by.

The majority of the population has lived for years in isolated communities of just a few thousand, and this isolation has had a profound effect on the Norwegian character. Over the centuries, Norwegians have developed a deep dislike of crowds. They are consumed by a desire to be alone whenever possible. Country folk rarely travel to the city, and city folk spend hours at the weekend

> **66 Isolation has had a profound effect on the Norwegian character. They have a deep dislike of crowds. 99**

driving to isolated areas where they can be on their own in the unspoilt nature.

Alone is best

The Norwegians are not social people and social situations make them feel uncomfortable. This is because social situations require small talk – an alarming prospect for a Norwegian. Dread of it only dissolves once a Norwegian has consumed a large quantity of alcohol, but government regulations ensure this occurs very rarely.

The desire for solitude means that relationships are clearly categorised and Norwegians keep large parts of their life secret from others. Friends are reserved for enjoying hobbies with and most Norwegians have different friends for different hobbies. Colleagues remain in the workplace and it is extremely rare for a Norwegian to invite a colleague over for dinner. For a Norwegian, the ultimate good time is hiking 12 hours up a mountain with a trusted friend in total silence. When they reach the top, they will share a cup of coffee from a flask, speaking only to say how nice it is to be alone. They will then turn around and hike down for another 12 hours. Every Norwegian home features at least one framed photograph, taken from the top of a mountain, with two friends standing side-by-side and a stunning view of unbroken countryside behind them. If busy city life gets too much, they can look at this photograph to remember better, more silent, times.

> **❝ The ultimate good time is hiking 12 hours up a mountain with a trusted friend in total silence. ❞**

Pragmatism

Years of hard work in frozen and isolated fishing and farming communities have ensured that the entire population of Norway takes an extremely pragmatic approach to life. Even sex must have a practical purpose. It is a way to produce children and pass the time on long winter nights. It is not something to get excited about.

Norwegians can find a practical solution to almost anything. Cyclists manage to keep cycling despite the ice and snow in winter by putting studded tyres on their bikes, while skiers keep skiing in the summer by putting wheels on their skis. And when the authorities made smoking in public places illegal, smokers responded by turning to *snus*, chewing tobacco that a Norwegian can place under his top lip whenever he needs a nicotine fix.

The entire country is run with a pragmatism that others may marvel at. When the county of Vestfold decided to recycle as much waste as possible – including organic rubbish, glass, metal, paper and plastic – it realised that the population would only fully comply if the refuse was picked up from outside their house. Each house now has five different coloured bins, one for each type of waste, and a calendar on the wall showing which rubbish is collected on which day.

Most new roads are paid for by tolls levied once the road has been completed, and these are removed once the road has been paid for. To

❝ Even dogs are often forced into jackets with reflective strips. ❞

increase road safety during the long winter nights, local councils give out *reflekser*, small reflective discs that adults attach to their clothes and backpacks when they are out and about to make them more visible to traffic. Children are given full reflective vests that they wear over their coats, and even dogs are often forced into jackets with reflective strips.

Of course, not everything runs smoothly all the time. Toll stations are left in place long after the road has been paid for, the reflective vests for children are nearly always four or five sizes too big, the kitchens of Vestfold are overflowing with different types of trash and the Norwegians' mouths have been turned brown by *snus*, but these are minor grumbles compared to the challenges overcome.

Perhaps the most famous example of Norwegian pragmatism is Roald Amundsen's journey to the South Pole. While Sir Robert Falcon Scott may be known for his heroic failure, it was Amundsen who got there first – and returned alive. That he did so is a testament to Norwegian pragmatism. While Scott refused to eat any dogs who had died from the cold because he could not bring himself to eat an animal he had become friends with, Amundsen not only ate his dogs, but planned to do so from the start.

> 66 For a Norwegian, a problem is simply a challenge to overcome. 99

Yes, you can!

Norway is a land of unerringly happy and positive people and the country is regularly near the top of the World Happiness Index. Even the most daunting problem does not seem to dent this aura of positivity. For a Norwegian, a problem is simply a challenge to overcome, and failure is just another chance to try again. If a Norwegian sees a mountain, he will believe that he can climb it. If he sees a recipe, he will believe he can cook it. If he sees a business opportunity, he will believe he can grasp it. It's not that a Norwegian puts doubt and negativity aside; these thoughts simply do not enter his mind.

This can be quite disconcerting for a foreigner. Ask a Norwegian if it's possible to walk from the ski town of Voss to the city of Bergen, and the Norwegian will say yes. He will not think to inform you that the walk would take around three days.

Even the extreme cold in the country does not seem to dampen the Norwegian spirit. The Tromsø International Film Festival is held in January and regularly includes out-

66Even the extreme cold in the country does not seem to dampen the Norwegian spirit. 99

door screenings despite average winter temperatures in the city of -6°C. The locals simply don an all-in-one winter suit, pack a flask and head out to be enter-tained. These outdoor screenings are often the most popular at the festival, which indicates that Norwegians prefer the challenges of sitting in sub-zero temperatures to the comforts of a warm air-conditioned cinema.

Norwegians even reflect this positivity onto the people they meet. Tell a Norwegian that you can dance, and you might well find yourself on stage two weeks later playing the lead in a local production of Aladdin and His Lamp. Even if you perform terribly, the crowd will give you a standing ovation because

Norwegian audiences are so positive about what they see, they deal exclusively in standing ovations.

Such positive thinking is easier than you may imagine in a country that boasts one of the world's richest and best functioning welfare states. In Norway, the tax rate will make your eyes water, but you get a lot for your money: unemployment benefit rivals a decent middle-income salary in most other nations, healthcare is free and of a universally high quality, and pensions are generous. Even prisoners in high-security jails live in conditions that would make the residents of old people's homes in most other countries green with envy.

> **66 In Norway, the tax rate will make your eyes water, but you get a lot for your money. 99**

The huge safety net spread under the feet of the whole nation means you would have to work extremely hard *not* to live well in Norway. If you do manage to fail at everything and your life falls apart, the Norwegian state will find you a place to live, offer to retrain you, give you psychological counselling and pay you a decent salary while you find your feet again. It's as if every Norwegian has a third, extremely well-off parent who will always look after him, however badly he discredits the family name.

Because failure never has dire results in Norway, every Norwegian has a BIG PLAN that he is waiting to put into action. He may be planning a charity walk around Asia, dreaming of building a new house or looking to start a new business. He may even have all three plans in development at the same time. But do not be surprised if years later nothing has actually been done. The important thing in Norway is to believe you can do something. Doing it is another thing entirely.

The inner Viking

Almost every foreigner associates Norwegians with the Vikings. However, anyone coming to Norway expecting to see marauding tribes with horned helmets and swords and daggers will be disappointed. Norway is one of the least Viking-like countries in the world. It is calm and well-managed, and the people are decent, shy, polite and practical. But Norwegians are still proud of their Viking heritage and there is a suppressed Viking inside every one.

This hidden Viking sees the light of day when a Norwegian is alone (which is often) and

> 66 Norwegians are still proud of their Viking heritage and there is a suppressed Viking inside every one. 99

deep in the sanctity of nature. He can then scream out loud, kill fish with a knife and skin a deer, free from the weight of modern social niceties. At these times, there is no need for small talk. It is the only time a Norwegian can relax.

The international inferiority complex

Once the Vikings fell from power, the other Scandinavian nations moved in. From 1397 to liberation in 1905, Norway was ruled from afar by either the Swedes or the Danes.

Today, Norway is an important player on the international stage. The country has money from oil. They give out the Nobel Peace prize and have respected peace negotiators and statesmen. But the centuries of being the lowest of the low in the Scandinavian pecking order have left a mark.

66 **The centuries of being the lowest of the low in the Scandinavian pecking order have left a mark.** 99

Deep down, the Norwegians have a sneaking suspicion that this international recognition is undeserved. This is reinforced by the manner in which the Norwegians got their oil. According to the Danes, the Norwegian Minister of Trade, Jens Eversen, did not play fair during the negotiations to divide up the North Sea. Legend has it that he got his Danish counterpart intoxicated at the start and the Dane then signed away the oil-rich Ekofisk oil field without considering the consequences. Although most historians agree this story is not true, it still leaves most Norwegians with the nagging feeling that they got more than they deserved.

Scratch any Norwegian, and you will find an inferiority complex as deep as the Norwegian fjord they grew up beside. Ask any Norwegian, even an Olympic champion, if they can ski, and they will reply with a shrug, 'Yes, a little.' Tell a Norwegian that he has done something well, and he will smile, thank you politely, and then point out a technical flaw in what he did. Explain to a Norwegian how well you think his country's trains run, and he will reply through gritted teeth, 'Things run better in Sweden.'

Attitudes & Values

Janteloven

In Norway, everyone is seen as equal and every person as equally important. This basic principle underpins the entire society, and affects everything from tax rates to family relationships.

> **There is huge social pressure to be as similar to everyone else as possible.**

There is huge social pressure to be as similar to everyone else as possible. It's not that non-conformity is frowned upon; it simply isn't done. If a man makes a scene in a café, the other customers will make one of three assumptions: he must be foreign, temporarily unhinged, or both – and everyone will ignore him until he shuts up or goes away.

This social pressure was first put into words by Aksel Sandemose in a book about life in a fictional

town called Jante which was governed by laws (*loven* =
the law). These laws are written as ten commandments
which all town inhabitants must follow:

1. You're not to think you're anything special.
2. You're not to think you're as good as [the rest of] us.
3. You're not to think you're smarter than us.
4. You're not to convince yourself that you're better
   than us.
5. You're not to think you know more than us.
6. You're not to think you're more important than us.
7. You're not to think you're good at anything.
8. You're not to laugh at us.
9. You're not to think anyone cares about you.
10. You're not to think you can teach us anything.

Although Sandemose was a Dane writing about
Denmark, he wrote the book in Norway and the deep-
rooted social attitudes that he describes are seen by
Norwegians to be equally applicable to Norway as to
Denmark. However, the interpretation is different
between the two countries. In Denmark, the core of
Sandemose's *Jantelaw* is that no-one can consider himself better than anyone else and, if he does, he will be
quickly brought down to earth. In Norway, anyone can
consider himself better than anyone else, as long as he
considers everyone else to be equally good.

This may seem like a contradiction, but to
Norwegians it makes perfect sense. Anyone who

succeeds in Norway will be admired, as long as he immediately shares his success around, for the good of the community and Norway in general. Ole Gunnar Solskjær, for example, a Norwegian footballer who won the Champions League with Manchester United in 1999, is more revered in Norway for establishing football training academies for children after his retirement than for his footballing prowess.

Jantelaw governs how Norwegians act in a whole variety of situations. If you spend your hard-earned bonus on a brand new sports car, your neighbour will only be pleased for you once you have offered to drive his daughter to handball practice in it. If you are lucky enough to land a contract importing a new type of ski boot to Norway, you would be foolish to announce to your friends

> 66 Norwegians love taxes so much they even called them treasure (*skatt*). 99

'I'm going to be rich!' Instead, you should carefully explain the details of the deal, before demonstrating how it will provide jobs for the local community, improve the medal haul of the Norwegian ski team at the next Winter Olympics and enable you to open the ski retreat for underprivileged children that you have always dreamed about.

This goes a long way towards explaining the Norwegians' love of taxes. Norwegians pay some of the highest taxes in the world. They love taxes so much, they even called them treasure (*skatt*).

19

A Norwegian often makes jokes about high taxes but he rarely complains because tax is seen as a way of sharing wealth. However, this must be done fairly and, as a result, the Norwegian tax form has become one of the world's most baffling pieces of paper. To fill it in, you need to spend hours making complicated calculations related to the size of the loan on your car, the value of your house and your anticipated income from work, savings, fishing and land use.

> **❝ While a Norwegian often makes jokes about high taxes, he rarely complains because tax is seen as a way of sharing wealth. ❞**

To ensure Norwegians dedicate the necessary time and effort to their tax form, the government publishes every individual's tax statement. The newspapers use the information to search out and name and shame any individuals who haven't paid enough. To find out if your neighbour/son/colleague is complying with *Jantelaw* and pulling his tax weight, simply search for his name and address on the tax authority's web site.

Community action

Despite their intense craving to be alone, the Norwegians understand that their nation can only survive with community action. This fact causes them something of a problem, but the Norwegians are nothing if not practical and they have come up with a solution called *dugnad*. A *dugnad* is a day when everyone in the community agrees to set aside their dislike of socialising in order to get together for the greater good. *Dugnads* are organised regularly to clean up communal housing, the village green, the local kindergarten or anything else that the community has a stake in. Everyone is expected to take part and not attending a *dugnad* is seriously frowned upon.

For many Norwegians, a *dugnad* is the only time they get together with their neighbours. During the *dugnad* they work side by side, eat together, and may even make brave attempts at small talk. However, as soon as the *dugnad* is over, the neighbours will return to their separate lives, and to wishing there was no-one else around.

> **During tho *dugnad* neighbours work side by side, and may even make brave attempts at small talk.**

Dugnads are so successful that the town of Larvik managed to organise a week-long *dugnad* to renovate its waterfront. The result was a beach complex (including swings for kids, picnic areas and volleyball courts) large enough for the entire town to enjoy without having to mingle too closely with anyone else.

The Norwegian concept of community action spreads to events as well. Everyone is expected to help out with preparations for Norwegian National

Day, the school play, the Christmas market and other communal events. Guests are even asked to bring food to birthday celebrations. This is done with the Norwegian's usual focus on practicality, so do not be surprised if your invitation includes the name of the dish you are supposed to bring along. When you arrive, give the dish to the host, and collect the empty plate or bowl (which will have been washed by one of the guests) when you leave.

Equality

Because society in Norway places a high value on equality, especially between the sexes, feminism has long been a dead term to most Norwegians, simply because it is no longer relevant. The proportion of women in government has remained at roughly 45%

66 In the family, mothers and fathers are equal parents. 99

since the 1980s, no-one bats an eyelid at a female boss – unless they are extremely attractive – and women occupy a number of high profile positions. In the family, mothers and fathers are equal parents. Fathers, just like mothers, change nappies, drop children at kindergarten and make packed lunches – and both parents go out to work.

Norwegian workplaces also support equality between the sexes. As parents you get one year of parental leave to split between you, ten extra sick days every year in case your child is ill and everybody leaves work at 4 pm on the dot. If you stay in the office after 4 pm, you are not viewed as a dedicated employee; you are deemed to be a bad parent. If, however, you explain that you are leaving early in order to take your daughter to ballet class, your colleagues will simply say '*Ha det gøy*' (Have fun).

Yet Norwegian men are still men and Norwegian women are still women. Most parents split parental leave so that the father takes only three months off and the mother takes the rest, and while a Norwegian father may be happy to take his children to kindergarten, he will usually have at least one work-related conversation on his mobile phone while getting them into their playsuits. Even parental duties seem to divide naturally along gender lines. The mother chooses the clothes, makes the dinner and remembers birthdays and dental appointments, while the father ferries the young to sports classes and takes them on their first hunting trip.

> **"If you stay in the office after 4 pm, you are not viewed as a dedicated employee; you are deemed to be a bad parent."**

This sense of equality is applied equally to minorities and immigrants. However, the immigrant must also be seen to be pulling his weight, and will quickly be ostracised if he does not learn Norwegian, comply with *Jantelaw* and take part in *dugnads*.

Green is best

Unsurprisingly for a nation so devoted to nature, the Norwegians are determined to protect the environment. Apart from the five separate bins at home, bins in the cities and public buildings are designated for different waste types and a Norwegian will dutifully carry an empty paper cup around town until he finds the right receptacle. When buying bottled or canned drinks in the supermarket, you pay for the drink as well as a deposit for the container. Norwegians save these containers in yet another bin at home and trudge to the supermarket once a month with a plastic bag clinking with empties. This behaviour is so ingrained that a Norwegian with a plastic bottle abroad will carry it back home to Norway in order to dispose of it correctly.

> **66 A Norwegian will dutifully carry an empty paper cup around town until he finds the right receptacle. 99**

In the few houses where segregated rubbish is not collected, the homeowner will load his plastic, paper and metal into the back of his car every other Sunday and drive to the recycling station outside the town. Considering that the car is usually a fuel-guzzling SUV and the recycling station is invariably at the top of a winding mountain road, this excursion probably does more damage to the environment than good. But then Norwegian environmental concern stops when it comes to energy consumption.

Unlike their Danish and Swedish cousins, the Norwegians consume energy as if it was going out of fashion. Lights and appliances are left on at home, computers are left running at night, solar panels are few and far between and a Norwegian homeowner will happily heat his terrace during the long winter nights so he does not get cold when he pops out for a ciga- rette. Even towns put heating under major pavements and squares in order to keep them clear of snow and ice during the winter. The government is try-

> **" Norwegians believe in the right to own a high-powered car in much the same way as Americans believe in the right to own guns. "**

ing to curb this excessive fuel use – on the roads, at least – by introducing low tax rates for hybrid cars, and free parking and free refuelling for electric ones. But it will be many years before Norwegians give up the right to drive a high-powered petrol car. Norwegians believe in the right to own a high-powered car in much the same way Americans believe in the right to own guns.

The carefree consumption of fuel is justified by Norwegians because the country gets most of its electricity from hydropower. Most fjords have at least one power station nestled at the neck of the rivers that feed them, and electricity is cheapest in the spring when the melting snow makes the rivers run fastest. (And, even though the country is one of the world's largest oil producers, most Norwegian oil and gas never touches mainland Norway. The oil is processed on floating production and storage vessels and the gas is piped straight to the UK and Europe.)

The fact that Norway's wealth comes from a fuel source that is destroying the planet is a painful truth for the nature-loving Norwegians. They deal with this pain in much the same way that a mafia heiress may deal with the origins of her fortune. They forget about it whenever possible and continue to enjoy the money. Norwegians work the oil fields and service the oil platforms, while sweeping their reservations firmly under the carpet.

The EU

The Norwegians spent 400 years as a Danish colony and then a century in a 'union' with the Swedes, and the word 'union' still makes them shiver. When the European Community became the European Union in the early 1990s, the Norwegian Eurosceptics could hardly believe their luck – their slogan had always been 'No to a Union' and suddenly their marketing was being done for them.

66 They spent a century in a 'union' with Sweden, and the word 'union' still makes them shiver. 99

Since then Norwegians have twice rejected EU membership, but the country has still implemented more EU directives than any actual EU member state. This contradictory behaviour stems from the fact that Norwegians believe all other nations to be less responsible than themselves. Ask a Norwegian about the EU and he will tell you that he likes the EU and the principle of community behind it, but he does not want to share Norwegian oil money with the rest of Europe, especially those bottomless pits in *Syden*.

Religion

Norway is a Protestant country: over 70% of the population belong to the Evangelical Lutheran Church of Norway. Most of the believers are in the south east of the country where, as well as the state church, there are a large number of independent churches and religious communities based on Lutheran doctrine.

However, according to a Eurobarometer Poll, only around one-quarter of Norwegians believe in God. For a Norwegian, church is essentially a four-time event. He will go for christenings, confirmations, weddings and funerals, but everything else is a stretch too far. Why go to church on a Sunday, when the sun is shining and the ski slopes are calling?

Of these events, confirmation is by far the most extravagant. A celebration that a child has successfully reached his or her 14th year, confirmations are planned months in advance. The seating has to be carefully thought through, the flower decorations arranged and new outfits bought specially for the occasion. For the child in question, the new suit or dress may be uncomfortable and long speeches from distant relatives boring, but this is compensated for by the gifts. Every guest has to bring something and the child will end the day with a number of new gadgets as well as a significant amount of cash.

Confirmations take place during late spring and early summer and are so popular that a Norwegian may end up with no free Sundays in May. Even atheists want to get in on the act and have developed the humanist confirmation, which is essentially the same, but requires no contact with the church.

> 66 The average Norwegian believes in hard work before play and has a regulated approach to indulgence. 99

Despite this general lack of belief, Protestant values still underpin the country. The average Norwegian believes in hard work before play and has a regulated approach to indulgence. A Norwegian parent, for example, will only allow his children to eat sweets on Saturdays. On this day of the week, he buys a massive bag of chocolates, jellies and other candies and his children wolf them down. They then run around like kites until bedtime, high on sugar, confirming the parent's belief that sugar intake should be strictly controlled.

Family Matters

Norwegians are raised in small villages nestled deep in the fjords or on small islands (there are more than 50,000 along the coast, of which 2,000 are inhabited). Here they experience an idyllic childhood of skiing, fishing, hiking and swimming – and travel to the family hut every weekend to do the same activities in greater isolation. They play

> **66 Norwegians experience an idyllic childhood of skiing, fishing, hiking and swimming. 99**

on their local handball and football teams and build lasting relationships with other children in the village.

At the age of 18, a Norwegian leaves the family home and heads to the big city to further his education, build a career and find a mate. This usually involves working hard during the week, and drinking hard every Friday and Saturday evening with the express purpose of becoming sufficiently uninhibited to start a conversation with someone of the opposite sex. These alcohol-assisted conversations eventually lead to a relationship, the relationship eventually leads to co-habitation, and co-habitation eventually leads to children. More than half the children in Norway are born out of wedlock, and living and breeding with your *samboer* (cohabitant) is an officially recognised status.

Cities are very child friendly with small playgrounds every few houses. These give the children a place to play with others in the neighbourhood, and the parents get a good work-out while carting their kids from one playground to another so that they get a well-rounded play experience.

Children are only raised in the city until they are a few years old. As soon as the first child is born, a Norwegian couple begins the delicate negotiations of deciding whose small village they will move back to in order to settle down properly. Invariably, the woman wins, unless the man happens to inherit the family farm. The couple then buy a house down the road from the woman's parents, get married to formalise their parenting arrangement and raise their children. Once a child turns 18, he will move to the big city – and the cycle begins again.

> **The family house is more a central hub than a home.**

The family home

The family house is more a central hub than a home. It's the base from which Norwegian families can plan their trips to the countryside, prepare their lunch boxes and take a quick break between activities.

Houses, like everything else in Norway, are designed with practicality in mind. The roofs have ladders attached to the tiles so the chimney sweep, who is paid for by the local council, can easily access the chimney. All rooms have wooden floors which are easy to wipe when snow and ice drip on them from outdoor clothes, and every bathroom has underfloor heating to keep toes warm when it's -20°C outside.

Norwegian homes are packed with the latest flat screen TVs, espresso makers and computer consoles, but interior design is something of an afterthought, if it is thought about at all. If you know that outside your window you have the most spectacular countryside, why bother paying for beautiful curtains when all they will do is get in the way of the view?

Childcare

The state takes considerable interest in the welfare of children and does all it can to encourage young Norwegians to contribute to the gene pool. There are, after all, only 5 million Norwegians in the world and more are needed if Norwegian culture is to survive. While working couples get extensive parental leave, the benefits also extend to unemployed pregnant women who get a lump sum that is roughly equivalent to 1.5 times the monthly average wage just before the birth of a child. And all parents receive a small sum per child per month which helps keep growing children kitted out with clothes.

> **66 The state does all it can to encourage young Norwegians to contribute to the gene pool. 99**

To ensure that parents do not have to give up their careers, children start in state-subsidised kindergartens around their first birthday. Norwegians firmly believe that not going to kindergarten is detrimental to the child. As families are generally small and access to extended family is limited by the distances involved, kindergarten is seen as the first step in integrating a child into Norwegian society. Children are looked after by trained staff who teach them to play together, eat together, sing together and resolve differences through dialogue. And, true to the Norwegian spirit of experiencing the great outdoors, they spend at least one day a week traipsing through the woods in their oversized reflective jackets, whatever the weather.

66 The reliance on kindergartens has given rise to a Norwegian phenomenon: the child commuter. 99

The reliance on kindergartens has given rise to a unique Norwegian phenomenon: the child commuter. Legally, every municipality must guarantee a place in a kindergarten for every child. But municipalities are large and the competition for centrally located kindergartens is fierce. This can result in a child ending up in a kindergarten that is over an hour's drive from home, which means the parents have to load their offspring into the car at 7 am, drive one hour to kindergarten and then one hour back, and then do it all again in the afternoon. The solution is to drop your children at the home of a local *dagmamma* (day mother), a middle-aged woman who, having given her best years to raising her own children, is now earning an extra few thousand kroner a week by looking after other people's.

Learning the hard way

Norwegian parents do not believe in forcing their off-spring to do endless hours of homework, nor do they like video games and other temptations of modern culture. Children, they think, will best develop their character by early confrontation with the harsh Norwegian nature. Every Sunday during the winter you will see hordes of families travelling in a line across fields and tracks on cross-country skis, with the father setting the pace at the front and the four-year-old struggling along at the back. The bribe for the kids is a hot chocolate in one of the numerous communal huts that are dotted along the ski and hiking routes, and a chocolate covered wafer bar named Kvikklunsj ('Quick Lunch').

❝ The bribe for the kids is a hot chocolate in one of the numerous huts along the route. ❞

Kvikklunsj has based its entire marketing strategy on this ritual. The ads on TV show hardy Norwegian families stopping for a break in their marathon Sunday outings and contentedly sharing a Kvikklunsj between them. And every bar has a recommended hiking or skiing trail on the packaging.

The Norwegian attitude to child-rearing is different from the other Scandinavian countries. If a four-year-old falls from a climbing frame and hurts himself, a Danish mother will rush over and spend the rest of the day comforting her son. A Swedish mother will immediately write to the municipality and demand that a committee is formed to recommend changes in the design of the playground. A Norwegian mother won't have to do either: her child will not be in the playground because he is too busy bivouacking in the woods.

> **66** Norwegian colonies on the Spanish coast are created to be just like a slice of Norway, but with better weather. **99**

The elderly

As Norwegians grow old they begin the long pilgrimage to retirement in *Syden*, normally somewhere in Spain. The Norwegian colonies on the Spanish coast are created to be just like a slice of Norway, but with better weather. The shops stock Norwegian newspapers, food and filter coffee, so retirees can enjoy a Norwegian breakfast on the balcony overlooking the Mediterranean, and all the apartments have large satellite dishes that pick up the latest episodes of *Dagsrevyen* (the longest-running news programme on

Norwegian television.) The Norwegians living in *Syden* return home twice a year – for Christmas and for 17 May.

When they get too old to look after themselves, elderly Norwegians return to Norway. But they do not return to the bosom of their family because their children are too busy ferrying their children between football and handball games to look after them. Instead, the old are stored in one of the numerous state-run retirement homes, where they can grow senile in comfort, eating boiled fish with boiled potatoes every day. They are wheeled out on 17 May to wave their flags and then forgotten about again for the rest of the year.

> **Parents have a habit of combining two first names that have no right to go together.**

Names

Very few Norwegians have middle names, but parents have a habit of combining two first names that have no right to go together, and you may well meet an Odd Magnus, Inger Alice, Ole Harry or Lars Jacob. Ever searching for equality, younger Norwegians are adopting the Danish and Swedish trend of combining the parents' surnames when they marry. You are therefore increasingly likely to meet someone called Odd Magnus Hansen-Stjernberg. What happens when

Odd Magnus Hansen-Stjernberg decides to marry Inger Alice Haug-Johansen is a conundrum for the next generation to solve.

Naming children is strictly governed. It is illegal to give a child a name that could be detrimental to it,

> **66 It is illegal to give a child a name that could be detrimental to it. 99**

and names must already be in common use. If you wish to choose a more unusual name, you have to apply to the local council, giving written evidence that the name has been used by your family before.

First names are usually from Old Norse (such as Solfrid or Ingeborg for girls and Oddgeir or Åmund for boys), or Christian saints and apostles. At one time it was common to give children, especially boys, English names. However, for some reason these children do not seem to have fared as well as their peers – Norwegian jails are populated by men called Kevin, Ronny and Johnny – and the trend is dying out. No-one uses nicknames. If you are visiting a prison and an inmate introduces himself as Ronny, do not call him Ronald in an attempt to be more formal.

Norwegian surnames are usually patronymic. This is done with the addition of *sen* (son), hence the most common are Hansen, Olsen and Johansen. There are also plenty of surnames that are influenced by Norway's abundant nature, such as *Berg* (mountain), *Vik* (bay) and *Haug* (hill). Many also end in *gård* (farm) and Ødegård (abandoned farm) has been common since the bubonic plague.

Manners & Behaviour

The Norwegians are, essentially, a decent and polite people. However they can come across as rude. This is because they view politeness as an unnecessary social interaction and try to avoid it. Norwegians appreciate directness in speech and spice their sentences liberally with (often English) swearwords. It is considered perfectly acceptable to swear – even on television –

> 66 They view politeness as an unnecessary social interaction and try to avoid it. 99

if you have the right background. Union bosses and artists swear liberally to demonstrate their proletarian upbringing, the Oslo middle-class do not, and if you were born in the North, swearing is regarded as part of your cultural heritage.

Eye contact and conversations with strangers are avoided which is why, if a Norwegian bumps into someone in the street, he will not apologise. Apology opens up the possibility of a conversation, and as no Norwegian wants to enter into a conversation unless he absolutely has to, starting one without just cause is far more impolite than bumping into someone. If a guest at a Norwegian dinner party reaches across you to get the salt, he is not being rude, he simply believes that asking you to pass the salt is an imposition on you when, with a little effort, he can reach it himself.

This makes Norwegian service polite and efficient, but never overbearing. A waiter will only talk to a customer long enough to find out what he wants and will deliver it as unobtrusively as possible. However, with Norway's rising financial clout in the region, the likelihood of being served by a Norwegian in Norway is decreasing. In a neat historical role reversal, Swedes – once the ruling class in Scandinavia – now travel to Norway in their hordes to find well-paid seasonal service work. Norwegians never tip, mainly because Norwegian cafés and restaurants pay their waiting staff a decent wage.

> 66 Norwegians view queues in much the same way as sprinters view the starting blocks. 99

Greetings

Norwegians are not big on greetings. Both men and women shake hands when they first meet but, unless they marry, this will be about the only physical contact they ever have. However, a change is taking place and women may now hug when they meet. Some men are following suit, but the Norwegian man-hug is more a show of strength than a greeting and is usually a painful experience for the smaller of the two.

Queuing

Norwegians view queues in much the same way as sprinters view the starting blocks. When waiting for public transport, a Norwegian stands in an orderly manner until the bus comes into view. He then springs to life and charges towards the front of the queue, barging his way on regardless of whether or not someone wants to get off.

Punctuality

The Norwegians are a punctual lot and the idea of being fashionably late is looked upon as a bad foreign habit. Therefore, if you arrange for your daughter's birthday party to start at 1:30 pm, expect to have a full house by 1:45 pm. Punctuality is applied to both the beginning and end of arrangements, and invitations regularly have both a start and an end time. If your daughter's party is scheduled to end by 5 pm, your house will be deserted by 5:01 pm. The only time that this does not apply is meetings, which will go on until everyone has expressed their opinion and a consensus has been reached.

Driving

Norwegians love to drive. Every household has at least one car, and a simple way to shock a Norwegian is to tell him that you don't have a driving licence.

Yet the state does all it can to make driving as unpleasurable and costly as possible. Roads have tolls, the tax on a new car can amount to more than 100% of the cost of the car and petrol prices are among the highest in the world, even though the country is one of the world's biggest oil exporters.

Norwegian speed limits are painfully low. The national limit is just 80 kilometres an hour, and any road that goes remotely near a house will have a limit of 50 kms an hour or less. To ensure Norwegian drivers stick to these limits, speeding fines are based on a percentage of your income and can be higher than the fines given to people caught with small amounts of Class-A drugs.

> **66 Indicating is viewed as an optional extra by everyone except the authorities. 99**

How well you obey the law depends on where you drive. A Norwegian driver will blithely ignore the limit on winding mountain roads, cruising up behind any Sunday drivers and passing them on near-blind corners. Yet, on the few stretches of motorway with a speed limit of 110 kms an hour, the same driver will cruise at a steady 108. Indicating is viewed as an optional extra by everyone except the authorities, and a driver who indicates on a roundabout simply has to be a Swedish or German tourist.

Norwegians are required by law to use special tyres in winter. Those living in the mountains have studded winter tyres, and need to pay an extra road toll every time they drive them into the city because of the extra wear and tear to the roads. Changing tyres twice a year is hard work, so most garages open on Saturdays in the autumn and spring and will change your tyres for a small fee. Some garages even run 'tyre hotels', and will store your summer tyres for you during winter, and vice versa.

> **66 Norwegians love talking about the cost of buying and renovating their mountain hut. 99**

Pedestrians have right of way on Norwegian roads and there are no rules for bicycles. A Norwegian will happily launch himself and his family onto a pedestrian crossing without looking to either side. City drivers, therefore, drive extremely slowly, with their eyes as much on the pavement as the road ahead.

Money talks

It is considered impolite to ask a Norwegian how much he earns. This is not because he will not want to tell you, but because it is an unnecessary attempt at conversation. Everyone knows how much everyone else earns because they have already checked on the government tax website. Nevertheless, Norwegians love talking about money, particularly the cost of buying and renovating their house, mountain hut or boat. Most of these conversations focus on just how expensive everything is – because everything really is expensive. Foreigners are shocked by prices in Norway, particularly for food and drink. Buying a round of drinks for four people can cost the equiva-

> **66 Buying a round of drinks for four can cost the equivalent of a return air ticket. 99**

lent of a return air ticket, which will most likely cause any new-comer to exclaim loudly and make comparisons with the cost in their own country. The Norwegian will have heard all this before, but will secretly enjoy being reminded of the one benefit of living in such an expensive country: when he goes on holiday, every-thing will be cheap, especially the alcohol.

Obsessions

Practical clothing

No matter how long you are in Norway, even if you are just changing planes at Gardermoen Airport in Oslo en route to somewhere else, someone will tell you that there is no such thing as bad weather, just bad clothes. This phrase is repeated whenever anyone complains of being cold or wet – which happens a lot.

In the winter, temperatures remain in the minus 20s for weeks and even months on end, especially in the Arctic Circle or in the mountains inland. Even on the West coast, where temperatures are considerably milder, the weather is ever present. The city of Bergen holds the record for the most days of consecutive rain in Europe. In 2007 it rained every day for 90 days. Taking a practical view of a dire situation, the locals saw the breaking of the record as a chance to celebrate, and the local paper, *Bergens Tidende* (*The Bergen Times*), ran a rain update on the front page every day as the milestone approached. There was even some disappointment when the skies cleared on day 91 – and something close to desperation when it began to rain again on day 92 and then continued for another three weeks.

Dressing to beat the elements gives a Norwegian a great sense of pride. TV news reporters, for example, will only interview people indoors if the sun is shining. If a storm is raging, the interview will take place outside, usually with the office of the interviewee in clear

66 Dressing to beat the elements gives a Norwegian a great sense of pride. 99

view behind them, which demonstrates to the viewers just how sensibly both the interviewee and interviewer are dressed.

Norwegians put practicality before everything else when choosing their clothes. A Norwegian will cheerfully turn up for a date dressed in ski trousers and a heavy hiking sweater. The only time you will see him dressed in anything other than practical clothing is when he is going to a wedding, funeral, Christmas party or communion – in which case he will wear his *bunad* or a brand new suit with muddy hiking boots.

National costume

The *bunad* is the Norwegian national costume and is worn on any festive occasion where formal dress is

> **66 *Bunad* shops offer tailoring services to let out the seams as the years add up. 99**

required. Each town or region has its own *bunad* and most date from the 18th and 19th centuries. When you buy a *bunad* and its accompanying hand-made silver and gold jewellery you buy it for life.

The Norwegians' obsession with the *bunad* is as much to do with practicality as national pride. A *bunad* never goes out of fashion and is forgiving to bulges. To accommodate growing waists, *bunad* shops offer tailoring services to let out the seams as the years add up, and take them in again when the *bunad* is passed down to the next generation.

Kon-Tiki

Thor Heyerdahl set out from Peru in 1947 with a small crew on a hand-built raft called the Kon-Tiki. For three and a half months its journey across the Pacific Ocean gripped the world until it arrived in the Tuamotu Islands in Polynesia, after a journey of 4,300 nautical miles. Heyerdahl's journey re-wrote traditional anthropological thinking, proving that it was possible for the ancient peoples of South America and Polynesia to have had contact via the sea.

After Kon-Tiki, Heyerdahl made more rafts and more journeys. He wrote papers, conducted archaeological digs and developed theories about the ancient world, from the Pyramids in Egypt to burial mounds in the Maldives. He died in 2002, but his legacy lives on. Heyerdahl represents everything Norwegians love about being Norwegian. He was an adventurer and explorer

66 Thor Heyerdahl represents everything Norwegians love about being Norwegian. 99

who honed his survival skills in the harsh Norwegian mountains. He was a loner who organised others towards a common good. He was an engineer who overcame any problem put in his way. He was a popular scientist who stood up to the snobbery of the scientific community. He was a nature-lover who took on nature and beat it time and again. He was a Viking for the modern age.

The cheese slicer

The cheese slicer is seen as the one essential item in everyone's home that foreigners have yet to appreciate. Invented by carpenter Thor Bjørklund in 1927, the cheese slicer is shaped like a small spatula. Its metal head has an open slot which cuts thin slices when dragged across cheese.

Open a kitchen drawer in any home, hut or communal building and a cheese slicer will be the first item you see. Norwegians even have an ornately decorated cheese slicer for special occasions.

A Norwegian would find life without a cheese slicer intolerably hard, and anyone who is planning to leave the country for more than three weeks will include one when packing. There is also an intense desire to share this fantastic invention with the rest of the world. You can find cheese slicers in the gift shops in almost every airport in Norway, and they are regularly given as presents to visiting foreigners.

> **66 Brunost (brown cheese) is the growing-up taste that Norwegians never grow out of. 99**

One reason that the cheese slicer has never taken off internationally is that it only works on Norwegian cheese. Using it on Brie will lead to severe clogging and Cheddar will crumble rather than slice. This is perhaps why the two most popular cheeses in Norway, Norwegia and Jarlsberg, have such a rubbery consistency.

The ultimate Norwegian food experience is to eat *brunost* (brown cheese), sliced with a cheese slicer, on an open sandwich. *Brunost* is the growing-up taste that Norwegians never grow out of. When a Norwegian takes a bite of *brunost*, he is immediately transported back to an idyllic moment in his childhood, when he sat happy, exhausted and silent with his family after a hard four-hour hike, looking out over a fjord with the sunshine on his face. To a Norwegian, *brunost* is the taste of bluebells, dappled sunlight and mountain streams. To anyone else, it's most peculiar. It is sweet in flavour and sticks to the inside of your mouth like glue.

Cod liver oil

Norwegians believe they are the healthiest nation in the world. This is not because they exercise four hours a day and eat nothing but boiled food. It is because of cod liver oil.

For a Norwegian, cod liver oil is the elixir of the gods. Packed full of Omega-3, it contains all the essential goodness

66 Norwegians truly believe that cod liver oil will extend one's life by a number of decades. 99

of codfish and Norwegians truly believe that it will extend one's life by a number of decades. Every household has a bottle tucked in the fridge door and a mother will spoon it down her children once a day before taking a swig herself directly from the bottle. Ask a Norwegian if they like the flavour and they will shrug. Liking or disliking cod liver oil is not something a Norwegian considers. He has been drinking it from the age of four weeks and will continue to do so until he reaches the grave.

Eating & Drinking

When it comes to food, bland is best. Norwegians like their food boiled and a typical evening meal will consist of boiled fish, boiled potatoes and one other boiled vegetable. In fact, the verb cook (*koke*) also means to boil and the word for a cook (*kokk*) has the same roots. This gave rise to one of the most famous diplomatic faux pas in Norwegian history. The story goes that a Norwegian Ambassador and his wife had been invited to dine with the President of an unnamed South American country. Upon tasting the food, the Ambassador's wife exclaimed, 'I must congratulate you, Mr. President, on the quality of your *kokk*.'

> 66 When it comes to food, bland is best. Norwegians like their food boiled. 99

Fast food

Norwegians think of eating in much the same way a racing driver thinks of a pit-stop. Meals are simply a way to refuel before getting back to more important activities.

The day starts with a rapid breakfast of cereals with milk or yoghurt. Lunch is a quick open sandwich. The evening meal is served early, normally around 5 pm, and the young are made to eat another quick meal before they go to bed.

No evening meal is complete without potatoes.

Originally introduced to Norway in the 18th century by 'potato vicars' – enlightened men who travelled the Norwegian fjords and mountains teaching poor farmers how to grow them – the humble potato soon became the Norwegian staple. Inexplicably, the Norwegians have never cottoned on to the fact that potatoes can be fried, roasted, mashed or served in any number of ways. Instead, they boil the living daylights out of them.

Perhaps driven by a desire to escape their mother's boiled meals, younger Norwegians have moved on to more sophis-

> **❝ If Norwegians view food as fuel, then coffee is the oil that keeps the engine running. ❞**

ticated flavours. Today, the most popular meal in Norway is the Grandiosa, an oven pizza that is as far removed from the Italian concept of pizza as a pizza can be. Most Norwegians love it. Dubbed 'laziness in a box' and 'refrigerated evil', some 24 million Grandiosas are sold each year and supermarkets dedicate acres of freezer cupboard space to displaying ton upon ton of its seven different varieties.

Meals are accompanied by a cold drink (water, milk or fruit squash) and followed by a coffee. If Norwegians view food as fuel, then coffee is the oil that keeps the engine running. Norwegians drink more coffee per capita than any nation, bar Finland. Every office has an industrial-sized coffee machine that pumps out a constant supply for the workers, and every household has at least two coffee machines, one a fancy espresso maker and the other for filter coffee. But a Norwegian will drink any coffee he can get his hands on. He has no qualms about drinking day-old coffee from the bottom of a percolator pot.

Eating outside

The only time Norwegians get real pleasure from eating is when they are outside. As soon as temperatures creep above freezing, a Norwegian will don his knitted jumpers and windproof jacket and head to the mountain, park or beach to eat. Much of the time, these outdoor meals involve nothing more complex than bread with *brunost* washed down with filter coffee from a flask, or a can of cold beer and a few sausages cooked on a disposable grill. But the food is not the point. The point is to take a moment from your busy life to feel the sun on your face.

66 The only time Norwegians get real pleasure from eating is when they are outside. 99

The best foods to eat outside are waffles, and their savoury equivalent, sausages. The delicious Norwegian waffle is made from a thick batter and served warm with jam and cream. You can find a waffle stand at every event in Norway, from ski competitions to flea markets, normally manned by two teenagers out to make an extra few kroner with their mother's waffle iron.

In summer, thousands of Norwegian families head out every weekend to pick the abundant blueberries and cowberries that grow all over the country. The children stuff the berries straight into their mouths and end up with fingers and faces stained dark red from berry juice. The adults collect them in plastic pots and take them home to make smoothies, jams and desserts. For a Norwegian, finding an area thick with berries that has not yet been pillaged is one of the ultimate feel-good moments of the year.

> 66 When Norwegians want to get back to their Viking roots they eat *lutefisk*. 99

Lutefisk

When Norwegians want to get back to their Viking roots, normally at Christmas or on 17 May, they eat *lutefisk*. Perhaps the most unpalatable food in the Western World, *lutefisk* is made from dried white fish, usually cod, steeped in lye (*lut*). The lye gives it such a high pH value that the fish becomes caustic and would most likely corrode the plate if it was not soaked in water for six days before being served. *Lutefisk* has a jelly-like consistency, a surprisingly mild flavour and an intensely offensive odour. Not even a Norwegian can eat it without the aid of at least three glasses of strong liquor, usually aquavit, which makes some suspect that eating *lutefisk* is simply an excuse to get rip-roaring drunk.

Restricted alcohol

Alcohol consumption in Norway is low compared with the rest of northern Europe, just 7 litres per person per year when in Sweden it is 8.7, in Denmark 10.2 and in the UK 12. However, it may not appear that way, because Norwegians tend to consume their entire year's quota in one night. Walk into the centre of any Norwegian town on a Friday or Saturday evening and you can see many a normally quiet and reserved Norwegian hanging from a lamppost.

> **66 Alcohol consumption in Norway is low compared with the rest of northern Europe. However, it may not appear that way. 99**

A trip abroad is another chance to drink to excess. No matter how early the flight, a Norwegian will celebrate his new-found freedom by having a beer before take off and a whisky on the plane. He will hit the bar as soon as he lands and drink for the entire time he is away – not because he wants to, but because he can.

Due to the population's inability to consume alcohol sensibly, the state has taken matters into its own hands – so buying alcohol takes careful planning and a considerable budget. Wine and spirits can only be bought at state-run *vinmonopolet* (wine monopoly) stores (open Mon-Fri 10–6 pm; Saturday no later than 3.00 pm). This, plus shockingly high prices, means that smuggling and moonshine production are thriving industries. Exploding moonshine equipment is one of the most common causes of fires, especially in the North where drinking is viewed as the best way to keep out the cold.

Leisure & Pleasure

Most nations can be split into two groups: country folk and city folk. For Norwegians, the split is slightly different: country folk and country folk who are unfortunate enough to live in the city. This is because there is nothing more important to Norwegians than enjoying the great outdoors. Happily, they have a lot of outdoors to enjoy.

Norway covers an area of nearly 400,000 square kilometres and if the Norwegian population spread themselves out equally across the country, a person would have to walk 300 metres to meet someone else. (Compare this to England, where you would bump into someone after just 10 metres.) In the vast majority of the land,

66 There is nothing more important to Norwegians than enjoying the great outdoors. 99

the 300 metres would stretch across wilderness, and covering it would involve kayaking, rock climbing and abseiling. Fortunately, nearly every Norwegian not only enjoys these antics, but is also proficient at them.

The simple life

Norwegian city folk have this open countryside within easy reach. You can take a tram from central Oslo to Nordmarka, a wooded wilderness where you can quickly lose yourself among the rocks and trees. In Bergen, it is almost impossible to drive for more than ten minutes without finding yourself halfway up a mountain. However, for most Norwegians just being in the countryside is not enough. They also need to be as far away from any other human being as possible.

66 For most Norwegians, just being in the countryside is not enough. 99

This desire explains the popularity of Norwegian hut culture. Every weekend, thousands of Norwegians depart the city in their SUVs and drive for four or five hours along ever narrowing mountain or coastal roads until they reach Norwegian nirvana: the family hut. This is generally a small wooden structure with two bedrooms and a wood stove.

The traditional hut has no electricity and an outdoor toilet, typifying the Norwegian desire to truly get back to nature. However, the less hardy generations brought up with the conveniences of electricity and flushing toilets have started to demand modern comforts during the weekend as well as during the week. Today, most huts have running water, underfloor heating and satellite TV. (Most TV suppliers offer 'house and hut' packages that mean you can get your favourite soaps and sitcoms in your house and your hut from the same supplier.)

Despite this, the Norwegians still view the hut as the best way to spend the weekend in perfect isolation surrounded by beautiful nature. The more

> **66 The more inhospitable and isolated the place, the stronger the Norwegian's desire to build a holiday hut there. 99**

inhospitable and isolated the place, the stronger the Norwegian's desire to build a holiday hut there. Unfortunately, this view is shared by countless other Norwegians and most huts are surrounded by hundreds of other huts, full of Norwegians desperate to get away from everyone else.

Pleasure with a purpose

Foreigners brought up with the belief that relaxing involves lounging on the sofa may find leisure time in Norway a challenge. The Norwegians believe that any leisure time must be enjoyed actively, preferably in the abundant countryside. (If, for some reason, you can't make it to the countryside, a trip to the gym or a game of football or handball are acceptable alternatives.)

In the winter, Norwegians relax by going on 10-hour ski trips through the woods. In the summer, they relax by exhausting themselves hiking, kayaking, sailing and swimming. In the spring and autumn, they relax by carrying equipment for hours into the wilderness in order to hunt and fish – and then wear themselves out hefting their catches back home.

To express the many different ways that you can experience nature, they have invented hundreds of phrases and words using the word *tur*, which means trip or tour. Norwegians go on a *topptur* (walk to the top of a mountain), *bærtur* (berry picking expedition) and *hyttetur* (trip to a cabin). They eat *turmat* or *tursnacks* (any food that is consumed while out in nature).

> **They relax by carrying equipment for hours into the wilderness in order to hunt and fish.**

The granddaddy of all *tur* phrases is *Ut på tur, aldri sur*. Its literal translation is 'Out on a trip, never sour', but the actual meaning is closer to 'Get your lazy ass outside where the fresh air will combat the modern illnesses that plague contemporary society and contribute to the worsening of our collective emotional, physical and psychological health.'

Skiing

It is said that Norwegians are born with skis on their feet. While this may be medically impossible, it's hard to disagree if you happen to visit a Norwegian ski resort. Children as young as three ski as if it's the most natural thing in the world, performing tricks and jumps, and whizzing past any Danish or Swedish skiers who happen to be cluttering up the slopes.

Due to their expertise on skis, Norwegians continually have to find ways to challenge themselves on the slopes. Nearly every town has its own ski jump and the local children dream of representing Norway at the Olympics. Telemark skiing is also popular. The original version of downhill skiing invented in the county of Telemark, this type of skiing requires skis with special boot bindings. Turning involves bending one of your knees almost to the ground and is almost impossible for a non-Norwegian.

> **Children as young as three ski as if it's the most natural thing in the world.**

Many Norwegians enter annual Birkebeiner races. (Birkebeiner was the name of a powerful Viking tribe.) The longest of these lung-busters is 54 kms and takes in three major mountain peaks. This is not challenging enough for most Norwegians, however, so competitors must also carry a 3.5 kilo backpack. A popular TV show involved a group of immigrants to Norway training for a Birkebeiner. Most had never been on skis before, and Norwegian viewers marvelled at their inability to master such a simple skill.

The right equipment

No Norwegian would ever undertake any activity – be it business or pleasure – without the right equipment. The right equipment must be of the latest kind and have all the bells and whistles. It must also be perfectly prepared before any activity. Waxing skis correctly is seen as being as important as skiing itself, cleaning sails is as important as being out on the water.

> **66 Waxing skis correctly is seen as being as important as skiing itself. 99**

All this preparation takes a lot of time. To ensure this doesn't lead to an imbalance between maintaining equipment and using it, Norwegians tend to focus on day-long activities. A Norwegian will not just go for a walk in the woods; he will prepare his equipment, pack food and the items needed to cook it, find the latest maps of the area and then embark on a 12-hour hike during which he can truly enjoy all the equipment he has taken with him.

The only exception to this is if the Norwegian is trying an activity for the first time. In this case, he may borrow the latest equipment from a friend. However, the preferred choice would be the equipment his great-grandfather used when crossing Greenland in 1923.

Hunting

There are 1.3 million guns kept in Norwegian homes, approximately one per household. A relatively high percentage of people know how to handle guns due to military service, and there are almost as many shooting ranges in Norway as there are ski jumps.

In spite of this, the murder rate is low (5 per million people each year, compared with 9 in the UK, 15 in France and 48 in the US). The high density of guns does, however, make Norway a chronically unsafe place for wolves, bears and other endangered animals. The government wants to conserve wildlife, but sheep farmers have other ideas. Whatever the authorities say, some animals are dangerous, and shooting them is both practical and fun.

There are strict laws on shooting game and hunting seasons

❝ There are almost as many shooting ranges in Norway as there are ski jumps. ❞

are generally observed. If you like game meat and know a Norwegian hunter, invite him to dinner at the right time of year and, instead of flowers or a bottle of wine, he may arrive with freshly killed reindeer.

Cross border shopping

Like pretty much every nationality with high disposable incomes, the Norwegians love having the latest gear. This means they do a lot of shopping – even if they can't afford it. The average Norwegian has at least two credit cards, as well as debt on his house, hut, car and boat – and a morbid fascination with other people's struggles with debt. One of the biggest hits on Norwegian television is *Luksusfellen* (*The Luxury Trap*), a reality show in which debt-laden couples agree to hand over control of their desperate finances to two financial experts. The couples are usually hundreds of thousands of kroner in the red, with no hope of paying off their loans, and have a huge pile of unopened bills tucked inside a cardboard box. The high point of the programme is when the box is opened and the level of debt revealed. For the audience, the pay off is seeing someone who is deeper in debt than they are.

66 **Norwegians have a morbid fascination with other people's struggles with debt.** 99

Despite the public's desire to shop, most retail businesses close at 5pm on weekdays and 3pm on Saturdays. Government regulations also restrict opening on Sundays, which makes the average Norwegian town feel like a ghost town for one day of the week. This, combined with eye-wateringly high prices, makes the border run a popular activity. Every Saturday, thousands of Norwegian families pile into the car and cross the border into Sweden – a veritable shopping Valhalla. Compared with what the Norwegians pay at home, the prices are rock bottom.

For those unfortunate enough to live on the wrong side of the Oslo fjord, ferries run to Strømstad in Sweden four or five times a day at weekends, transferring people in empty cars out of Norway, and people in cars packed with meat and cheese back again.

The quotas for meat and cheese are clearly displayed on government notices inside the boat and terminal, but this is one of the few regulations that Norwegians are happy to break. The chance of getting caught by customs is minimal – they are too busy trying to catch the people who drive meat and cheese into Norway by the lorry load.

DIY

In Norway the need to refurbish a bathroom is a time for celebration. It's a chance to get your tools out, roll your sleeves up and enjoy a weekend of serious DIY. Male or female, young or old, you are not only expected to be good at home improvement, you are expected to enjoy it.

Walk into one of the huge DIY stores clustered around the outskirts of town on a Saturday morning and you will see an entire cross-section of Norwegian society browsing the shelves for building materials. Young couples will be discussing which lights to choose for their kitchen, old men will be measuring bits of wood

66 In Norway the need to refurbish a bathroom is a time for celebration. 99

for new shelving units and well-dressed middle-aged ladies will be pushing trolleys filled to the brim with pipes for their plumbing.

Once you have the parts you need, the key is to start work confident in the belief that even if you muck something up, you can always hammer your way out of it. And, if something goes seriously awry, you can always ask a neighbour. In fact, your neighbour will appreciate being asked, because if there's one thing better than DIY, it's telling someone else how to do it. Your neighbour will also have all the necessary tools stashed in his basement along with a couple of old sinks, some unused kitchen cabinets and a broken chair he is planning to fix one day.

66 Your neighbour will also have all the necessary tools stashed in his basement. 99

If you visit his home and show interest in any particular fitting, he will explain to you how it was constructed and when. Then, the national inferiority complex being what it is, he will point to all the faults in its construction.

While Norwegians love getting to grips with a DIY job, there is a very practical reason for doing so. Norwegian builders, plumbers and electricians probably charge the most expensive day rates in the world. When you need to work three weekends of overtime just to afford a consultation with a plumber, you soon learn to fix a leaking tap yourself.

Culture

In Norway the arts are only practised by children and foreigners. By the time a Norwegian hits puberty, he will have given up dance, painting and music in favour of more productive pursuits like work, study and skiing. The last time an adult Norwegian went to the theatre was to see his daughter's end-of-term ballet performance – unless he is middle-aged, well-off and suburban, in which case he will have seen an opera performed by an Italian company at the only large theatre in town. Most towns in Norway spend their entire cultural budget on bringing in performers from abroad. As a

❝ In Norway the arts are only practised by children and foreigners. ❞

result, you can see quality performing arts in Norway, from opera to fado and tango, especially at the numerous international festivals organised around the country. However, the whole audience will have grey hair, and home-grown talent will be thin on the ground.

Painting and photography are the most popular arts. These are activities that Norwegians can practise alone, and they often combine them with their love of nature. Most towns of a reasonable size have one or two galleries that display landscapes by local artists and a photography club where enthusiasts spend as much time talking about gadgets and equipment as composition.

The Norwegians are openly envious of the culture produced by their Scandinavian cousins. They resent the Danes for their beautiful design and wish the Swedish pop bands that dominate the radio were their own. But they comfort themselves with the knowledge that Norway will top the medal haul at the next Winter Olympics.

Norwegian romantic nationalism

The golden period for Norwegian arts and culture was the second half of the 19th century. This was the time of Norwegian romantic nationalism, a movement that emphasised the aesthetics of Norwegian nature and was driven by the desire to escape the shackles of 'union' with Sweden. During this time, individuals set out to collect fairytales, folksongs and expressions from around the country to preserve and promote a sense of national identity. Officially, Norwegian romantic nationalism ended in the 1860s, but the movement had a profound influence on the artists that followed. Many went on to become famous around the world, but they had to escape provincial Norway in order to hone their artistic skills.

66 The golden period for Norwegian arts and culture was the second half of the 19th century. 99

Perhaps the most famous of all Norwegians is playwright Henrik Ibsen, best known for *Hedda Gabler,*

An Enemy of the People, and *A Doll's House.* Today, Ibsen is the world's most frequently performed playwright after Shakespeare. Although most of his plays are set in Norway – often in small towns reminiscent of Skien, the town where he grew up – he lived for 27 years in Italy and Germany, and rarely visited Norway during his most productive years.

The most famous piece of music to come out of Norway was written as incidental music for the Ibsen play *Peer Gynt.* Written by Edvard Grieg, *In the Hall of the Mountain King* represents angry trolls taunting the lead character and is recognised the world over – as is his Piano Concerto in A Minor (written in 1898) which captures the lyricism of Norwegian folk music.

> **❝ Ibsen is the world's most frequently performed playwright after Shakespeare. ❞**

The most famous painting, Edvard Munch's *The Scream,* was painted in 1893 and depicts the universal anxiety of modern man with its anguished figure against a tumultuous orange sky.

It was the intricacies of the human mind that fascinated author Knut Hamsun who is widely regarded as the father of the modern school of literature with his portrayals of everyday life in rural Norway (such as *Hunger, Mysteries* and *Victoria*). For many, Hamsun's legacy is tainted by his support for the Nazis, but his Nobel Prize for Literature in 1920 speaks volumes.

Other prominent Norwegians include another

Nobel Prize winning author, Sigrid Undset (whose masterpiece, the medieval epic *Kristin Lavransdatter,* has been in print for almost a century); Kirsten Flagstad one of the greatest opera singers of the 20th century; and Leif Ove Andsnes, described by the *New York Times* as 'the most accomplished pianist of the new generation'.

There are also innumerable sports stars and explorers, prize-winning chefs and the band A-ha who took the world by storm with their hit single *Take on me* in 1985. After breaking up and reforming any number of times, A-ha is still the biggest band in Norway.

Trolls and *nisser*

No Norwegian believes in trolls, but every Norwegian knows that they exist. This is due to a kind of cultural brainwashing started during Norwegian romantic nationalism and continued today by parents and kindergarten assistants. Romanticised fairy-tales feature trolls, *nisser* and a smart little lad called Askeladden – who always outwits the troll to win the princess and half the kingdom.

> **❝ No Norwegian believes in trolls, but every Norwegian knows that they exist. ❞**

Trolls live in woods, under bridges and in tourist shops, and are strong and stupid. *Nisser* are very small people and (usually) friendly. The most common is the *fjøsnisse*, a mischievous type who lives in farm out-buildings and looks after the animals. The *julenisse* gives the children presents on Christmas Eve.

Trolls and *nisser* have become deeply woven into Norwegian culture. They appear in books, in songs, on television and even in major motion pictures. They feature in knitting patterns and fabric designs, and statues of trolls and *nisser* decorate every Norwegian hut. If something goes missing, a *nisse* is usually to blame.

> 66 Norwegians don't have time to be funny. They are too busy waxing skis or improving their mountain hut. 99

Sense of Humour

To outsiders the Norwegian sense of humour is either crude or incomprehensible. Luckily, it's also rather uncommon. This is because Norwegians don't have time to be funny. They are too busy waxing skis, making packed lunches or improving their mountain hut so that it looks like a hut from the outside and feels like a modern apartment on the inside. These tasks are extremely time-consuming and certainly not things to be joked about.

If a Norwegian does stop long enough to make a joke, he will follow it with a loud laugh of his own. This is not because he finds the joke hilarious, it's because he fears that no-one will realise he's joking.

To succeed as a comedian in Norway you should preferably speak with a heavy regional dialect and side with simple folk. The man voted 'Norwegian comedian of the 20th century', Arthur Arntzen, is the archetype, performing as the stupid-looking North Norwegian fisherman Oluf. He cracks rude jokes about his wife, the weather and the silly authorities down South.

Self-deprecation

Most Norwegians will tell you that they share the British love of self-deprecating humour. They attempt to recreate this humour whenever they can. However, most attempts suffer from a lack of subtlety. When failing with a task, for example, a Norwegian may react by stating the obvious: 'I thought that was going to work. It didn't.' Realising this may be mistaken for a serious comment and not a joke, he will then laugh loudly.

> 66 Love of self-deprecation makes Norwegians very receptive to jokes about themselves. 99

The love of self-deprecation makes Norwegians very receptive to jokes about themselves. When a Norwegian finds himself talking to a foreigner, he will try to unearth all the things the foreigner finds funny about Norwegians. He will often tell a Norwegian joke to get the foreigner going. One of the best-known features the Norwegians' shy nature:

'How can you tell an extrovert Norwegian?'

'He's looking at your shoes and not his own.'

Some jokes have been integrated into the language. Norwegians will often refer to masters of red tape as a 'Soup Council'. In a famous television sketch from the late 1960s the inimitable Harald Heide Steen Jnr. plays the head of the National Soup Council who spends taxpayers' money and has a massive staff who do – well, hardly anything at all.

Killing whales for fun

In the 1980s most Norwegians who went abroad wore a T-shirt printed with: 'We kill whales for fun'. (The T-shirts also had a Norwegian flag on the arm, just in case anyone mistook the wearer for a Swede.)

At the time, the Norwegians were under intense pressure to stop whale hunting. But Norwegians see whale hunting as a part of their culture and do not like other nations trying to stop it. Many of them also think whale meat tastes good, and know that one whale can feed a lot of people. The T-shirt was a way to make a joke of the situation. But not everyone found it amusing, even if the Norwegian laughed loudly as soon as he saw someone's eyes scanning the slogan on his chest.

The Swede, the Dane and the Norwegian

Like many nationalities, the Norwegians like to poke fun at their nearest and dearest, in this case, the Danes and Swedes. Invariably, the Norwegian is the level-headed member of the trio, the Dane a tolerable side-kick and the Swede the buffoon. A typical joke of this type will run:

> The Norwegian, the Swede and the Dane made a bet about who could stay the longest in a stinky pig barn. They all went in at the same time. After only two minutes the Dane came running out. Five minutes later the Norwegian stumbled out. After ten minutes, all the pigs ran out.

Business & Commerce

Norway's chief industries are fishing, pulp and paper, aluminium processing and oil and gas. Many of these industries are situated in isolated communities along narrow fjords, where factories and processing plants are built close to waterfalls and hydroelectric stations. Small villages spring up next to each plant to house the workers, but many people still prefer to commute for hours each day rather than live in communities made up entirely of their co-workers and co-workers' families.

Norwegians have been big players in the shipping

industry for many years and, of the ten richest people in Norway, three are involved in shipping. Under price-pressure from Asia, it is on the wane, whereas fish farming is growing rapidly. Norwegians export a huge amount of fish and shellfish. Their salmon is known around the world, and king crabs are seen as the next cash cow by the Norwegian fishing industry.

> 66 It's actually impossible to avoid the oil industry in Norway. 99

Norway also excels in a number of niche industries. Mustad is known to anglers around the world for making hooks that fish love to bite. Dale of Norway's range of performance knitwear, including Teflon-coated wool to repel water, is favoured by hikers around the globe, and Madshus skis have helped cross-country skiers of all nationalities take Olympic gold.

But the true power behind the Norwegian economy is oil. Statoil, the state-owned oil company, is the nation's largest company and a large part of the Norwegian population works the oil rigs, develops software or produces undersea equipment for oil exploration. It's actually impossible to avoid the oil industry in Norway. Even if you work in the service industry, you will be enabling other people to work the oil rigs. In order for Mr. Hansen to dedicate more time to the search for oil, Ms. Olsen looks after his children at kindergarten, Mr. Johansen drives him to and from meetings in a taxi and Mrs. Berg cares for his mother in the old people's home. And every Norwegian pays into a state pension scheme that is guaranteed by savings in the Norwegian oil fund.

The work-life balance

The Lutheran work ethic ensures that Norwegians work extremely hard when they are in the office, but they expect a lot of time off. Norwegians get five weeks of paid holiday a year and most offices are deserted during July. Some even close for the entire month because there is no-one around to do anything.

The 8–4 work day is structured to give everyone the longest afternoon possible. Lunch breaks are condensed into half an hour and the ingredients for open sandwiches are laid out in the canteen so employees do not need to pop out for a bite to eat. The correct way to prepare your office lunch is to place a slice of cheese and salami on a piece of bread, top it with cucumber or red pepper, then eat it, open, with a knife and fork, while discussing work with your colleagues.

> **❝The 8–4 work day is structured to give everyone the longest afternoon possible.❞**

Promotion is based on merit and, as you move up the career ladder, you are expected to contribute more and more of your time to your work. But you are not expected to give up your long afternoons. Instead, a manager leaves the office at 4 pm to pick up his children, takes them on a two-hour hike and then reopens his computer once they have gone to bed.

Offices organise events for employees twice a year. The office Christmas party is a big affair at which everyone tries to stuff as much food and alcohol into themselves as possible until the free bar is closed at around 10 pm. In the summer, employees and their

> **For a Norwegian at work, job satisfaction comes before any other consideration.**

families are invited to enjoy a picnic in the great outdoors. Other than this, most Norwegians prefer not to fraternize with colleagues. Colleagues remind them of work, and work reminds them that they are not out in nature.

No need to complain
In Norway you are defined by what you do. Luckily, the rule of equality states that, just like people, all jobs are equal. Hence, a carpenter gets just as much respect as a doctor, and a kindergarten assistant is seen as equally important as a teacher. The only failure is to not have a job. Or, worse still, to have a job you do not like. For a Norwegian at work, job satisfaction comes before any other consideration.

Companies will do all they can to provide it, but ultimately attaining satisfaction is believed to lie with the individual. Complain to Norwegian friends that you do not like your boss, and they will tell you to get another job. Say that you do not feel you have enough responsibility and you will be told to go to your boss and demand more. This is made easier by the Norwegian approach to management.

All Norwegian managers assume that every employee will work hard (between 8 and 4), and they assume that the work will be good. Managers see very little reason to add incentives and rarely follow up to make sure an employee has done what he was supposed to. They pride them-selves on being approachable and expect their employ-ees to come to them with any issues, problems or new ideas, especially if they will improve job satisfaction. Norwegian managers are, therefore, constantly in meetings with employees demanding more responsi-bility – or a new chair or a desk with a better view.

> **66 All Norwegian managers assume that every employee will work hard and that the work will be good. 99**

The long meeting

Because everyone is equal in Norway, everyone's opinion is listened to and all opinions are viewed as equally important. This is as true at work as it is among friends. A junior sales rep will happily tell his boss exactly what he thinks of the boss's new sales plans, often without being asked. Far from being offended by this, the boss will (at least appear to) appreciate the employee's opinion – and may even consider a change of plan.

This can mean that quite simple decisions become extremely time-consuming and meetings go on until everyone has had their say. As a result, Norwegians judge the quality of a meeting on the length of time it takes, rather than the outcome. Ask a colleague how the meeting went, and he may well reply, 'Good. It was at least relatively short.'

> **❝ Norwegians judge the quality of a meeting on the length of time it takes, rather than the outcome. ❞**

Organisation

Norwegian offices are informal in both attitude and style. Most have sofas where colleagues can discuss work informally with their feet up. If anyone arrives in the office wearing anything more formal than jeans and T-shirt, everyone will assume that he has just been to a job interview at a rival firm.

The typical Norwegian work organisation is flat, with silos of highly skilled employees working under a single manager who reports directly to the CEO. This promotes the sharing of ideas and opinions up and down the organisation – but not across. Each silo sees its work as the most important and works in ignorance of what any other silo is doing. Working across silos is difficult because it involves meetings. Every person in each silo will want to attend, and the meeting could go on for days. Once the meeting is over, no-one will ever have time to put the plans into action, because they are too busy attending other meetings.

Customs & Tradition

Most Norwegian holidays, although religious in origin, are viewed simply as time off work. Apart from Christmas and Easter, all holidays are packed into the month of May, starting with Labour Day on 1 May and ending with Pentecost 50 days after Easter.

Christmas

Christmas (*jul*) is the biggest holiday of the year and it starts early. The dark snowy streets are lit with coloured lights and huge Christmas trees are placed on every square. In the lead-up, the family gets together to bake *pepperkaker* – a type of gingerbread spiced with pepper and cinnamon – in the shape of hearts, reindeer and Christmas trees and tins of *pepperkaker* are piled high in offices, schools and homes.

Pepperkaker baking is a serious business. The city

of Bergen hosts the world's largest *pepperkaker* city, complete with *pepperkaker* houses, bus stations, libraries and replicas of Bergen landmarks. It even has its own (living) mayor. When a drunken vandal destroyed Bergen's *pepperkaker* showpiece, the whole country frantically baked emergency *pepperkaker* in order to re-create the city from the crumbs.

The entire month of December is a countdown to the big day. Children get small gifts – sweets, pens, plastic cars and anything else parents can find in the bargain buckets at toy stores – as part of their Christmas calendar. Every office, sports club and association hosts a Christmas meal for its members.

On Christmas Eve afternoon, the family sit down together for a huge meal which varies depending on which part of the country you are from. Easterners prefer *ribbe*

> **66 In the lead-up to Christmas, the family gets together to bake pepperkaker. 99**

(pork rib), Westerners eat *pinnekjøtt* (salted lamb ribs steamed on birch twigs) and many in the North choose *lutefisk*. But while *ribbe* and *pinnekjøtt* are salty and *lutefisk* pungent, the vegetables on the plate are sure to meet Norwegian standards of blandness. This is followed by creamy rice pudding with a fruit sauce and washed down with copious amounts of aquavit. For added entertainment, an almond is buried in the rice pudding and whoever finds it gets a prize – usually a miniature marzipan pig.

Once the meal is over, the family hold hands around the Christmas tree and sing traditional songs. Then they move on to the serious business of opening presents. Presents are delivered by the *julenisse* (the Christmas *nisse*), who has more than a passing resemblance to Santa Claus and looks suspiciously like Mr. Olsen from next door.

Other holidays

Although it is not a day off, Midsummer's Eve (*sankthansaften*) is one of the biggest nights on the Norwegian calendar. In the North the sun never sets on this night, and even in the South it dips below the horizon just after midnight only to rise again an hour or two later. To celebrate this longest day of the year and to keep the sun's flames alive for as long as possible before the world turns towards winter again, Norwegians light huge bonfires, mainly along the coast, which are a magnificent sight from the sea.

> **To keep the sun's flames alive for as long as possible, Norwegians light huge bonfires.**

After a barbecue in the garden, people flock to the water in their thousands, especially in the South of the country. Hundreds of boats, from small sailing boats to pleasure cruisers, join together to create huge flotillas. Seafarers leap from one boat to the next to share a drink with the captain, and the entire experience is one of community, framed by the beauty of a low-hung sun and the fires on the mainland that mark the route home.

Easter (*påske*) is more about skiing than Christianity. The holiday falls towards the end of the ski season, when the snow is deep and the slopes bathed in sunlight. The temptation to ski is just too hard to resist. Norwegians arrange for as many days off work as they can and drive to their mountain cabins loaded with ski equip-

66 **Norwegian families ski during the day and then curl up in the evening with chocolate and a page-turner.** 99

ment. Easter is also associated with crime – not committing it, but reading books about it. Norwegian families ski during the day and then curl up in the evening with chocolate and a page-turner (often by Jo Nesbø, Norway's hugely successful 'uncrowned king' of crime fiction).

Fastelavn is roughly equivalent to Shrove Tuesday. On *fastelavn*, children in kindergartens and primary schools across the land eat cream-filled rolls and make *fastelavnsris*, bunches of birch branches decorated with feathers. As it coincides with carnival, kids spend the entire day in fancy dress.

Round birthdays (those ending in 0) are also big events, especially for anyone over 40. Employers present the birthday boy or girl with a gift, and families organise large formal meals, often in a restaurant or catered party space. The meal goes on for hours because every relative, friend and passing acquaintance feels the need to stand up and give a speech. Attend one of these parties and you will soon understand how Norwegians feel during long meetings.

The *russ* celebration

Apart from confirmation, Norwegians go through one other rite of passage before they become an adult. The *russefeiring* (*russ* celebration) is the final time that high school students can let their hair down before they go to university or work. The word comes from the Danish *rus*, but the Norwegians have added an extra 's' to separate it from *rus* (intoxication), which is ironic considering that the *russefeiring* is all about getting rat-arsed. The event takes place across the whole Nordic region, but the Norwegians have perfected it to a form of ritualised drinking and debauchery that even the liberal Danes regard as taking excess too far.

> **66 For three weeks students travel from one party to the next in buses and vans that blast music to the entire neighbourhood. 99**

It starts in late April when 18–19-year-old students, known for this period as *russ*, don special coloured overalls. For the next three weeks, they travel from one party to the next in decorated buses and vans that blast music to the entire neighbourhood. Everything culminates on 17 May when the *russ* parade through the streets, singing, shouting and spraying water over everyone in sight.

As well as overalls, *russ* wear caps with string dangling down to which they tie an item every time they manage a certain 'accomplishment'. These accomplishments are generally focused on getting legless or getting laid. Drinking a bottle of wine in 20 minutes earns a *russ* a wine cork, for example, while asking random people if you can borrow a condom earns you a condom. Other accomplishments include putting a 'For Sale' sign on a police car or spending the night on the beach. Every year, a number of students are hospitalised or even die due to the excesses. In the early 2000s, the authorities tried to limit the *russefeiring* by moving some exams forward to early May in an attempt to force students to revise instead of partying. But the change had no noticeable effect, apart from lowering the level of the exam results.

> **Accomplishments are generally focused on getting legless or getting laid.**

For a country with such constipated alcohol laws and a prudish view on sex, the *russefeiring* is something of an oddity. But a Norwegian parent just shrugs his shoulders and comforts himself with the belief that his precious teenage daughter is getting a lifetime's worth of drinking and wildness out of her system in one month.

Government & Systems

Unless driving on remote mountain roads or smuggling cheese into the country from Sweden, Norwegians obey the rules and always follow the system. This is not because they agree with the rules or believe the system to be perfect. It is because they realise that the rules and systems have been created to ensure society functions smoothly, and Norwegians pride themselves on living in a country where things work.

Political parties

Norway is a social democracy with a big S and a big D. More than 70% of eligible Norwegians exercise their right to vote in general

> **❝ The government is always a coalition, which suits the Norwegians down to the ground. ❞**

elections every four years and the government is generally considered to be doing what is best for the people, regardless of which political party is in charge.

With a multi-party system, Norway has so many that no one party can ever win enough seats to gain a majority in parliament. The government, therefore, is always a coalition, which suits the Norwegians down to the ground. Politicians have to remain polite to each other, as they never know when they will need the other politicians' support, and ruling the country is essentially the political equivalent of a *dugnad*.

The unroyal Royals

The Norwegian Royal Family is surprisingly like any other family in Norway. The parents are happily married, the son is married to a woman with a child from a previous relationship and the daughter has gone slightly off the rails – all of which only seems to add to the Royal Family's popularity.

Its members are also extremely down to earth. If you hang out in the right areas of Oslo, it is not uncommon to bump into Crown Prince Håkon perusing the Grandiosa selection in the local supermarket.

Crime and punishment

Norwegian police are generally trusted and cases of corruption and bribery are few. They do their duty unarmed – but always have a Heckler & Kock pistol and machine gun in their patrol cars just in case things get out of hand. There are two parallel police organisations. While the city policemen are much like their European colleagues, the countryside is made safe by *lensmenn*, or county sheriffs. As communities are so small, most policemen and *lensmenn* usually have a very good idea of who did not commit a crime and a pretty good idea of who did.

The prison system is built on the principle that it is more important to reform prisoners than punish them. And it is hard to argue with the results. Norway has one of the lowest re-offending rates in the world; just 20%, compared with around 60% in the US, 50% in the UK and 35% in Sweden. There is no death penalty – Norwegians shudder at the thought – or life sentence (the maximum sentence is 21 years).

Prison cells usually have televisions, computers and en-suite bathrooms, and inmates have access to a wide range of education and training courses. But prisoners do not have everything their own way. When Skien prison increased prices in the prison kiosk, prisoners were quick to register a formal complaint and demand the introduction of at least one other kiosk in order to provide retail competition.

Education

The Norwegian school system is not designed to enable children to make the most of their skills. Its express purpose is to create good members of society. Indoctrination starts early. In kindergarten from the age of one, a Norwegian child learns the values of sharing and equality. When he moves on to primary school, he is quickly taught to appreciate hard work over achievement. By the time he finishes compulsory education, he will have completed so many collaborative projects that he might feel his final grades are

66 From the age of one, a Norwegian child learns the values of sharing and equality. 99

84

based on group capabilities and not his own.

While the focus might not be on grades, Norwegian schools are generally very good and the education they supply is up there with the best. 37% of the population go to college or university, with many gaining a degree above Bachelor level. If you want to study something at university for which there is no course, the government will pay your tuition fees to study it abroad – and students who are tired of cold weather and bland food suddenly discover previously undreamed of interests in very obscure subjects.

Language

Norway has almost as many dialects as mountains, islands and fjords. Every Norwegian is proud of his dialect, even more so if it is only spoken by a few thousand people. He sees it as a connection to his roots and a reminder of the small island where he grew up. He is, therefore, disappointed when a foreigner tells him that all the dialects essentially sound the same, a beautiful sing-song language with as many ups and downs as the country where it is spoken.

Official languages
The belief in equality means there is no officially sanctioned spoken language, but the dialect spoken by

urban middle-class Norwegians from around Oslo is regarded as the de facto standard. There are, however, two official written languages. *Bokmål* ('book tongue') is closest to the Norwegian spoken in Oslo and is essentially Danish with sensible spelling.

> **❝ To ensure all official languages are used, there are strict quotas for television and radio. ❞**

Nynorsk ('new Norwegian') is an amalgamation of different dialects. Around 85% of the population use *Bokmål* as their daily written language, 5.5% use both *Bokmål* and *Nynorsk*, and 7.5% use primarily *Nynorsk*. Sami is also an official language in a number of municipalities in the North.

To ensure all official languages are used and understood, there are strict language quotas for television and radio. This makes watching TV a haphazard affair for immigrants to Norway who may discover their favourite foreign programme is subtitled in *Nynorsk*, a language they have never learned.

Ja

Norwegian has three more vowels than English (å, ø and æ) but you have to be Norwegian to hear the difference between them.

Norwegian is possibly the only language where a gentle intake of breath is an accepted phrase. If a Norwegian agrees with what someone is saying, he forms the first letter of the word *ja* (yes) in his mouth and then breathes in quickly, essentially inhaling the word. This allows him to signal his agreement without actually saying anything.

Norwegian English

Norwegian is based on Old Norse, a language brought to the British Isles by the Vikings, and English and Norwegian are very similar in grammar and vocabulary. Many English words, such as house (*hus*), talk (*tale*) and tree (*tre*), have their roots in Norwegian. In recent years, this cross-pollination has gone the other way, and a Norwegian will travel to town on the *buss*, stop at the *stasjon* and take out money with his *kredittkort*.

The Norwegians are very good at English and will liberally sprinkle their sentences with it. They might, for instance, suddenly drop 'take up the challenge' into a sentence without thinking. Or say '*Jeg* nail'*a det*' (I nailed it), only half bothering to translate the English phrase, or '*Det var skikkelig* obvious' (It was really obvious), even though there is a perfectly good Norwegian word for obvious.

The Norwegians' proficiency in English makes it very easy to be a tourist. However, they have a habit of responding in English to any foreigner attempting to speak Norwegian. As a result, many immigrants to Norway never learn Norwegian, but find that their English improves by leaps and bounds.

The Author

Freelance copywriter Dan Elloway was born and bred in the West of England. He threw in a promising career as an actor and performance artist to pursue a woman to Poland. When things didn't work out with her, he moved to Japan, then Sicily, then Denmark, before eventually settling in Norway. Having been rained on constantly for two years in Bergen, he relocated to Tønsberg on the East coast, an area of the country that is sometimes misleadingly described as the Norwegian Riviera.

Not being the outdoorsy type, he tries to avoid extended contact with the Norwegian countryside as much as possible – much to the consternation of the locals. Instead he spends his days writing in cafés. He has published three English language textbooks, and written numerous articles, brochures and advertising campaigns. He dances the tango whenever he gets the chance.

He has a Norwegian-Polish wife and Norwegian-Polish-British daughter, and often fails to understand what either of them is saying.

Xenophobe's®
guides

Available as printed books and e-books:

The Albanians	The Italians
The Americans	The Japanese
The Aussies	The Kiwis
The Austrians	The Norwegians
The Belgians	The Poles
The Canadians	The Portuguese
The Chinese	The Russians
The Czechs	The Scots
The Danes	The Spanish
The Dutch	The Swedes
The English	The Swiss
The Estonians	The Welsh
The Finns	
The French	
The Frisians	# Xenophobe's®
The Germans	## lingo learners
The Greeks	French
The Icelanders	German
The Irish	Greek
The Israelis	Spanish

Xenophobe's Guides

The Italians

Italians grow up knowing that they have to be economical with the truth. All other Italians are, so if they didn't play the game they would be at a serious disadvantage. They have to fabricate to keep one step ahead.

The French

To the French, there is a world of difference between rules and formalities. The former are to be ignored, the latter strictly observed. Everything must be done *comme il faut* (properly), from filling in a form to stuffing a duck.

The Americans

Americans are friendly because they just can't help it. But a wise traveller realises that a few happy moments with an American do not translate into a permanent commitment of any kind. This is a nation whose most fundamental social relationship is the casual acquaintance.

The Spanish

Anyone attempting to understand the Spanish must first of all recognise the fact that they do not consider anything important except total enjoyment. If it is not enjoyable it will be ignored.

The Greeks

The ancient sages carved 'Nothing in excess' and 'Know thyself' on the portals of the Delphic Oracle in an attempt to persuade their fellow Greeks to curb their emotions. They were not heeded then any more than they are now.

The English

The English share a dislike of anyone behaving in a manner that 'goes too far'. The admired way to behave in almost all situations is to display a languid indifference. Even in affairs of the heart, it is considered unseemly to show too much enthusiasm.

Xenophobe's® Guides e-books are
available from Amazon, iBookstore, and
other online sources, and via:

www.xenophobes.com

Xenophobe's® Guides print versions
can be purchased through online retailers
(Amazon, etc.) or via our web site:

www.xenophobes.com

Xenophobe's Guides® are pleased to offer a quantity
discount on book orders. Why not embellish an
occasion – a wedding goody bag, a conference or
other corporate event – with our guides. Or treat
yourself to a full set of the paperback edition.
Ask us for details:

Xenophobe's® Guides
e-mail: info@xenophobes.com

Xenophobe's® Guides enhance your understanding
of the people of different nations. Don't miss out –
order your next Xenophobe's® Guide soon.

Xenophobe's Guides